To Chris,

Best Wishes

Jennifer Lynch

WE HEAR YOU ANGELS!

Angel Wisdom

by

Jennifer Lynch

CONTENTS

Dedication

Remembering Susan with love

WE HEAR YOU ANGELS

ACKNOWLEDGEMENTS

Thank you to Julie Albion who created the fabulous cover for this book.

INTRODUCTION

This book explores how to make a connection to your Guardian Angel, as well as learning how to listen to your angel. It also looks at different types of angels as well as light beings. How by surrendering and passing your wishes up to the angels, is not the same as the Law of Attraction. It looks at archangels and my own angelic experiences. It helps you bring angels into your life with a realistic and balanced perspective. There are a few meditations or 'opening up' exercises which will help you to have a closer connection to the angelic realms, as well as clearing and balancing your energy fields. There are also channeled messages which I have received from angels, which explain about what's happening on planet earth at this evolutionary time. Why angels choose to be with us now through our transition, both as a race and as a planet. How angels come close to us in times of great upheaval both personally and universally. Why we find feathers and what this means. It asks, are angel feathers different to bird feathers? What makes them so special? I explain the need for us to become as balanced as we possibly can, particularly at this time of great upheaval. Why we are evolving and re-connecting to who we really are. We are both human and angelic. I explain about our chakra energies and the need to stay in the 'now moment' the gateway to the Uni-verse – our oneness or unity consciousness and more importantly your conscious self.

LISTENING TO YOUR ANGELS

Many of us have understood, from a very young age, that we have a Guardian Angel. But I wonder how many of us have grown into adulthood and still believe that we have an angel with us now, probably not many of us. So what happened in our lives that changed our minds? At what point did we stop believing that we are guided and protected by angels? If we would only wake up to the fact that we can still connect to angels in our daily lives and hear their gentle and encouraging words of wisdom, the world would be a different place. Many earthlings are totally unaware that we have an angel who is with us and will always be with us. This angel is assigned to us for our whole life and agrees to be our guardian. In my work as a therapist and angel card reader, I often see angels around people when they come to me for a reading. I have noticed that the angels are around people who are going through a particularly difficult time. The angels always come in very close around my clients. They often report to me that they are aware of angels and they have experienced feelings of being comforted. They too see angelic light or they say that they have been touched by the angels. Sometimes they discover white feathers left for them in times of need. So many of us are sensitive to these angelic energies but dismiss it, unless it's a time when we are in need of comfort. The angels appear to me as white light, which often sits around a person's shoulders or the energy of an angel might be standing by a person's side. Archangel Michael is at many sides. He appears with his sword of protection. He comes to us to give strength and direction. Angels gather around our heads and rest on our shoulders and sometimes touch people on the head, or blow softly. They make contact with us in many ways. So despite what you may think (rational mind), you are not shouldering your burdens alone because the angels do hear our requests. They help us by sending love and healing at difficult times. If you are a very sensitive person you may be aware of it. To say you need to believe in angels in order to feel their presence does contain an element of truth because to be 'open' to seeing and believing in them, will accelerate angelic experiences. But it is entirely our personal choice whether we chose to stay in the current vibration, or raise our energies to connect to other realms. There was a time when people accepted that our world was flat and if you travelled too far, you could fall off the edge! Your energetic world consists of 'the world,' that you yourself choose to create. Some people choose to become aware and others chose to be unaware of these frequencies. This doesn't mean that they don't exist! It means they exist beyond what is termed as 'normal' human perception! So are we ready for more dimensions? Are we ready to evolve to think that humans and angels can co-exist within the same time space reality? Are we ready to raise our vibration or frequency to accommodate more than what was written on the school blackboard? If not, then maybe this book isn't for you! For at first we have to believe, and then we see. Although occasionally, I believe that we break through without believing. An angel will appear right in front of us. From a personal point of view, I didn't believe in angels until someone said that Archangel Gabriel was standing at the side of me and helping me with my work. Another lady drew a picture of an angel standing behind me. It was confirmation for me of the feelings and messages I had already been receiving but I was still partly in denial until then. It was at this point in my life when I started to really feel angels around me. I felt their warmth, energy and comfort, and at times it felt as if they were holding me. The angels left me feathers in my darkest moments, which helped me to turn my life around. I saw huge round orbs and one day an angel came to speak to me from inside an orb! It sounded like a heavenly voice singing at a very high frequency. But how did all this start? It began with tiny flashes of blue energy – electric blue, like the sparks from Archangel Michael's sword opening up another sphere of reality. The unreal then became real to me and I was amazed!

One summer when my son was quite young, I took him to Cornwall to surf. At this time, funds were very low and I was travelling on a whim and a prayer. I had enough money to get by for food and camping for about four days but I had planned to be in Cornwall for a week, staying at a camp site near Newquay.

I left my son having a surf lesson because he felt quite comfortable with the guys who were taking him into the sea. They were going to teach him the basic techniques of how to stand up on the board. It was raining and quite choppy, and I was a little concerned about him going out too far. Still, the surf school was good and two men went out into the sea with the new pupils, one each side. Newquay, if you have ever been there, you will know that it is a very busy place and this particular summer was no exception. I wandered around the little tourist shops and decided to get a cup of tea. I looked in my purse. Funds were extremely low even lower than I imagined and I felt a sense of panic rise up inside me. I really didn't want to let my son down but what could I do? There would be maybe enough money left for two days, if I was lucky. As I stood in the queue in the cafe waiting to be served a cup of tea, I glanced down at the floor and I noticed a small white fluffy feather laying there. I was very surprised because it wasn't as if there was any other rubbish on the floor, or any indication that it had been dropped. Although I had checked by bank balance the previous day, I then heard a voice ask that I return to the Bank and take another look. I entered my pin and gasped, there was over £2000 in my account. Believe it or not I felt sick with shock! My first re-action was to queue up inside the bank and tell them that the money was not mine and there had been a huge mistake. So I went and asked who had made the deposit and I was told it was some kind of a rebate. Although I hadn't been expecting this, I was convinced it must be for me and I walked away dazed. At some stage later I found out that it was a mistake and it had to be paid back but not before we had made the most of our little holiday!

We drove down to Boscastle and decided to visit the Museum of Witchcraft! I thought the angels might be slightly displeased with this, but then again, I am a human! It's such an interesting place to visit, although parts of it (in my opinion) hold very powerful energies. I personally find it to be a little overwhelming, particularly upstairs but as a historical record, nonetheless very valuable. After a long and breezy walk up to the rocks near the sea, we eventually had a great slap on meal in a local restaurant. To be honest the whole experience was amazing! If you have never visited Boscastle go there! The energy of this place is incredible. We visited in 2006, after they had the flash floods in 2004. An unbelievable amount of water literally carried some of the houses away. There's a line to show people how high the water level rose in the museum. It's amazing that the people came back from it all and houses, walls, etc. had been rebuilt. Finally, I drove up the steep hill which eventually led us back to the camp site. It was one of my miracles and blessings I received from the angels and I thanked them! Thanking angels is very important and thanking humans is essential. There is much release of positive energy through gratitude.

RELEASING MEDITATION

Archangel Michael is a very special Angel. He gives us protection and we can call upon him in times of need and fear. I've explained more about him in more detail in the 'about the archangels section' later in this book. But, I would like to share with you a releasing exercise that I came across a few years ago. I have found this release very effective particularly at the end of romantic relationships, or for a situation where someone is taking a large amount of energy from you.

1. Close your eyes gently and visualise the person that you would like to detach from standing in front of you. Not too close but see them in your imagination.

2. Call in Archangel Michael to help you with his sword of light. Then see him making a figure of 8 around you and the person you wish to release.

3. Put yourself in one part of the eight and put the other person in the other part of the eight. See the figure eight as moving energy which is pulsating and sending positive vibes to you both.

4. Now ask Archangel Michael to break that figure of eight into two circles of light. He can do this with the tip of his sword

5. See the person you wish to detach from stepping away from you now with the circle of light still around them. See them moving towards the horizon until they become smaller.

6. See them disappearing over the horizon completely if you can. If this is hard, do not worry because in essence they are still gone. They are surrounded with light and they will remain protected.

7. You can finish this exercise with it is done, it is done, it is done because the power of three is very strong and sends a special energy out into the ethers of release.

What's happened is that you have broken the energetic link with that person or cord. You are now both free from any karma. You are both ready to move on with positivity. All soul contracts fulfilled!

This is a really good exercise. Although it is simple and doesn't take very long, I have found from my personal experiences and also from the experiences of my clients, that within a few days they began to feel very different. It restores your energy and in addition it allows you to move on. I told a lady about this exercise when she came to see me for a reading a couple of years ago, I had a wonderful surprise when she got in touch with me about three months later, by email, to say that she had used this exercise and it really worked for her. She felt so much better and she had been able to move forward from a situation where she was previously feeling stuck.

ASK YOUR ANGELS

Asking angels is really important. Although, I believe that it is unnecessary for us to repeat our requests over and over, just trust that they've heard you. Would you keep repeating your wishes to a human being? We sometimes do this but then it begins to fall on deaf ears. Angels are God's messengers and how you view or interpret God is irrelevant. A messenger is a messenger and angels work hard to bring our requests to the light. I am saying requests but equally we could say prayers or wishes. If you ask entirely for yourself, then it is unlikely that your wishes will be granted. However, if the request is for another, or for humanity as a whole, the angels will pass it up through the frequencies to a place where it will reverberate in the ethers in higher dimension time and space. If it really came from your heart – it won't be ignored.

That doesn't mean to say that you can't ask angels for help because they are here to help all of us. What I mean is that if you ask for help then you are passing it up to them to find the solution and for them to send love in the best way possible. Angels seldom answer requests which are not from the heart.

Is Asking Your Angels the same as The Law of Attraction?

The Law of Attraction is a magnetic energy field which resonates with all human beings on planet earth, if they choose to align with this vibration. Obviously, everyone would like to attract good things into their life. However, it's not the same as connecting to your angels. The Law of Attraction works though intent, or desire energy. If you are wishing to manifest blessings in your life such as a new home or a job, or perhaps a relationship then using methods to attract these things towards you is a great technique. I say technique because it involves taking the idea from your subconscious mind into the conscious and making it 'a reality.' I always tell my clients that it is a good idea to use a journal or vision board. If you are able to plan your goals by writing them in a journal, you then begin to make them conscious. You are then putting out a new frequency into the Universe or field of all connectedness, 'uni' being oneness! Much of our angst comes from separation, believing that we are alone on an island and that we're disconnected. Similarly if we are able to cut out pictures of our dream situation i.e. from magazines or old newspapers and place them on a vision board, be it a third dimension object of our desires, or a feeling, we're literally ramping up our attraction antenna! It means that we can attract the desired outcome by being within its resonance, instead of out of its resonance. In order to be within the desire resonance, we have to actually feel the thing we are asking for is real to us. To feel this, we have to engage with it. Manifestation is through the material plane of existence, which is within the realm of 3rd density or 3D. But the concept of manifestation is within the 4th density which means we can think it, but we have to 'will it' into our reality or accept it into being. With this there is also a certain amount of surrender but you are applying a mental imprint, or expectation of your desires into the magic formula. It's similar to a magician pointing his magic wand. He has to have the confidence to believe that his willing will change the course of destiny. Whereas, complete and utter surrender by asking the angels may feel as if it is a whole lot harder to accept. Taking action by projecting our thoughts towards our desires is a normal process for us, spinning the wheel and playing a part in our destiny. Whereas, the act of surrender, may well feel alien to us, due to our attachment to the physical and potential outcomes. In surrender, we don't have to ask for our number to come up, we have to communicate what's in our heart to a higher and more evolved part of us our angelic selves.

We need to trust in the outcome so that we can shine the light of our being into our new reality of space time existence!

BEING EARTHED

We are all connected in this vast matrix of energy which we call planet earth. In addition, we are all connected to the earth through the chakras on our feet and also through the earth's natural rhythms and cycles. We are predominantly creatures of the earth and when we are not earthed, we very soon begin to run into problems. It is common to experience feelings of floating, or not being fully in our body. We have to be embodied, within our body. The problem happens when our emotional field is out of alignment. This could be because we are experiencing a major life event such as a divorce or bereavement. When we are not aligned, we often experience a feeling of being 'all over the place' or as it's more commonly referred to 'all over the show!' To add to this, what we are currently experiencing at our current point in evolution is a kind of double matrix. There's what I shall call the 'matrix of human potential'. This is the one that when we experience it, the positivity which we encounter enables us to reach the highest part of us i.e. the divine, source, higher self (there are various words that people use to describe it). This is the energy which is our birthright. We know when we are connected to the divine because everything just falls into place. Things unfold with synchronicity and appear effortlessly. It could easily be described as falling on your feet, or just being in the right place at the right time, or even being given a golden opportunity! We may just bump into someone we haven't seen for a long time and they offer us a job. Or it could be that you meet someone who has a soul connection with you and you start a beautiful relationship. If you have had these experiences, then you were in some way connected to the energy of the divine matrix (or all that is). We can connect this way during meditation which is why meditation is so good for us. It awakens our true potential by helping us to align to our original blue print. In order for us to feel the benefits of these synchronicities we do have to stay grounded and in the now moment (in our body). We have to be in the observer rather than the observed because through our earth connection we are able to manifest blessings into our lives. The energy pours into our 'being' and feelings of being stagnant or stuck no longer exist.

What is a blue print?

A blue print is literally a map of your life. The plan you agreed to before you incarnated on planet earth. During our life time we have numerous opportunities to align to our blue print but the 'ego self' which has a powerful energy of its own, tries to pull us off course. By meditating regularly we can get control of the mind, or mad monkey ego self, the annoying voice which we want to still, or it can also be referred to as the inner critic. The voice that beats you up, brings you down, tells you that you are not this and that and prevents you living the bliss which was intended. With focus and positive intention though meditation, we can then start to integrate the parts of us that we left abandoned. Our soul fragments which have gone out on to other planes or existence and have remained stuck in those dimensions. Once we know who we are, why we are here and what is or isn't part of our blue print, we can stop wasting time on diversions. We can stop what they say 'barking up the wrong tree'. We can choose 'empower' instead of 'victim'. We have a map, we have a pointer and we begin to recognise parts of our journey. Perhaps the parts of our journey that we have done before and we now wish to continue. We can integrate who we really are and be in the soul, rather than be in than solely in 'the personality'.

But surely personality is a good thing?

Yes, of course it is. No-one is asking you to dump your personality heaven forbid! We all need a personality to survive in this dimension but we need awareness of our personality. We need to recognise what is ego and what is our authentic self. Can you imagine what the world would be like if we were all exactly the same and we all sat cross legged chanting day in day out. We need our differences and we need our ego but we do not need our ego more than we need our connection. Without ego we would not have enough drive to move forward. Ego is our identification. It's our name, it's our job. It is also how we differ to other people. It is in essence our facade, our mask or shadow. We can try and lose it like Peter Pan tried but without it we would soon start to feel a little lost. It wouldn't be long before we'd be begging to have our shadow re-attached! I often hear people say that they have killed their ego. Or use the words, death of the ego. Unfortunately, the ego never dies, not whilst we are here on planet earth. It sneaks up on us, tries to trick us by changing our personality and can drive us to addictions because it wants to be recognised. But the ego is still part of who we are. It's here to stay so we need to learn how to live with it. Not to fight against it. It's rather like having neighbours that you don't get on with. You can try ignoring them but you know they are still there and they may come back and annoy your twice as much. Best thing is to accept and surrender to a certain extent but ask for divine intervention! By surrendering and asking, you are creating a new possibility. So we have both the divine and the ego. In fact, one helps the other to grow and mature. It's a bit like man and a robot. If the robot became too powerful and started to govern the man, then sooner or later the man would become lost and would become a slave to the robot. The man has a soul and the robot doesn't but the man gave away his power to the robot and soon became a slave. This is akin to human nature – we easily give away our power, our sovereignty and who we are for something that we consider would be better. We can attract many things into our lives. We can attract positive things through will and intent and we can also attract negative things. This is done through 'the personality.' It's often a request made outside of ourselves and it isn't always divine by nature. You may well attract money, love, cars or relationships and these are all things that we as humans need, but you will only attract anything towards you at the level of integrity of your original intention.

If something is passed up the angels for help, we don't decide the outcome. It is passed through the vibrations to the source. As a result of this surrender, we may receive a blessing i.e. the vibration might change within us which balances the situation. Or someone may move closer to us or further away. Like I said, we don't have the power to decide the outcome. Rather, we have been heard and it's basically a matter of the energy shifting to make a new pathway. We have already agreed to this!

I was working several years ago for a woman who was making my life very difficult. She was a very controlling person. I can fully understand that she wanted the best person possible to work for her, but she took it upon herself to start interfering in my life phoning child minders for me, finding me suitable men to date and also she was withholding some of the hard earned money that was due to me, for a week in the future when she may not be able to pay me! I agreed to this because it was a seasonal job but of course, I then lived to regret it! At this particular time in my life, it was very difficult for me to find work having not worked for many years apart from bringing up two children and child minding! Although this job was not a good situation for me to be in emotionally, having some money appeared to be a better option than my other choice which I concluded at the time was struggling. However, I set out one morning on a damp day when it had been raining, along country roads. I was driving along country bends on the way to work and the road surface was wet. I suddenly noticed a huge cattle truck in front of me on my side of the road getting closer by the second. I glanced to my left to see if I could get over and at the side of me there was a huge grassy bank about six feet in height. As the lorry hurtled towards me at about 50mph, I realised that if he didn't move over there and then, he was going to hit me head on. At that moment which literally was a 'moment in time' I decided that if I was to hit the lorry if it caught me on the side of my car,

I might survive. I then turned the wheel full lock and left the road.

I'm not sure what happened then. I was told by a lady who was travelling behind me that my car flew up in the air. I totally believe it was angels that carried me over the other side of the road. I sat there dazed bruised and hurting. Diesel slowly started to pour out my car. The lady who was behind me approached me and talked to me through my window to see if I was alright and said she had called the ambulance for me. She didn't want to stay because she didn't want to be a witness! She told me that I would need to get out of the car soon because of the diesel. Unfortunately my knees hurt so badly that I couldn't move. Very soon a whole team of firemen came to cut me out of the car but they managed to open the door and I walked out. They insisted I shouldn't walk in case I had a head injury, but I hobbled to the ambulance. Remarkably when I got to hospital, although I was in extreme shock, all I needed was some strips put on one knee for one tiny cut. I remember hearing on the radio that it was miracle I survived. They were right, it was!

Shortly before I hit the lorry I saw my life run past me like a film strip. I was actually thinking that I had already had quite an amazing life. The other time I thought I was going to die, was when I swam too far out at

Walberswick. I got caught in the seas strong currents. I was thirteen and a very weak swimmer. The friend that I was with, managed to swim back but I just hung on to a beach ball which was floating further out to sea by the minute. I was terrified at the time because I didn't like and I still don't like deep water! Just before I hit the lorry, my thoughts flashed back to being in the sea, clinging hard onto that beach ball and I felt exactly the same feelings. At that time when I saw a life review, surprisingly, I also saw my life as whole and complete even though I was only thirteen. Then, in one conscious or NOW moment, I decided that I still needed to complete my life because there was still work to do, opportunities to be grasped and new directions to take. I gasped air and I grasped life. I knew that I had been touched by the angels as an amazing calm and yet decisiveness gave me yet another opportunity!

I left my job and decided that having not much money wasn't ideal but I wasn't up to going anywhere for a few months so it was fine. I preferred being with my children rather than persuading various friends to look after them in the holidays because they were still young. I decided I would take a new path. I would learn Reiki first and then I would train as a massage therapist. In the meantime, I would wait a while and then look for new work to keep the wolf from my door. I would do something a bit more fun where my boss didn't control my life, or telephone the men from the Telegraph to see if they had their own teeth or hair!

Previous to this accident, I had been told by someone in my spiritual development group, that if I didn't stop pushing myself, it would be taken out of my hands. It was divine intervention but not exactly the way I envisaged it. It was a lesson for me to listen because I was not listening to my angels at the time and they were screaming at me. Angels try to wake us up.

HOW DO YOU LISTEN TO ANGELS?

When I was a child I called it my conscience. Now I am an adult I call my inner voice, my guardian angel. Could this voice have always been my Guardian Angel? Yes, the angels assure me this is right. It was just that for many years, I didn't realise it. I didn't know that my conscience or voice (awake and awareness) was my angelic connection. I remember having a huge row with a friend of mine saying that angels aren't part of us and that they were God's messengers and nothing to do with me. But he insisted that angels were still part of us! Well if I saw him again now, I would have to say that I was sorry because I now feel that he was right. I believe that angels are part of us and part of the divine. They are messengers because they relay our messages to the higher or more evolved part of us. Like I said the lower aspect of us is very much third dimensional and is concerned about third dimensional pleasure such as money, identity, the physical body, gratification, sex mainly things that feed and satisfy the ego. Once you start listening to your inner voice (your angelic self) then you will find that certain things in your life become easy. Life is not easy when we ignore ourselves, or as Linda Goodman put it, your elves (that magic part of you, which makes you so special). So basically what I'm saying is that angels work inter dimensionally. They are angels in the higher dimensions, at the same time as supporting us in the third dimension. They come to remind us that we too are angelic. They could be described as our future selves who are awakening us to our full potential. Unfortunately, because the 'other matrix' (the illusion) we have partly forgotten why we are here. Rather like waiting for a bus and at the bus stop we know we are meant to be here for some reason but on another level, we know that the bus passed the stop long ago. We just failed to notice. The wiser part of us (our divine self) already knew that we were meant to let that bus pass us by. We sometimes need to forget in order to understand what we have to learn on planet earth, the mental and logical plays very little part in our spiritual connection. We are slowly re-learning and acquiring our soul memories once again through the innocence and purity of our inner child, who likes to explore, play and be peaceful. We are shifting not only ourselves into the fourth dimensional reality, but the earth is evolving too, through our intention! We, or at least many of us, here on planet earth at this time, have decided that enough is enough. We are fed up with duality (the self perpetuating state of being stuck in a hamster wheel) where situations keep repeating. We're now ready to move into a new frequency. We are tired of karma. We are tired of living out the illusions on planet earth. We have seen past the illusion of separation and we are ready to unite. We are ready to unite with our angelic selves once again. We wish to integrate all our missing soul fragments. We want to call that energy back to us, to feel complete and stop living a lie. We want the energy back which was robbed from us when we agreed to this massive 'experiment'. We have grown and we want to go home. We have incarnated on this planet now to tell others about this. Whether we are Crystal Children, Indigos or Rainbow Warriors, we are here to shift forward and now it's the time for this. We call upon the angels to help us because they know us intimately. Long ago they were a part of us and we are in many ways, still very connected to angels. They now wish for us to be re-united once again to work in unison with their energy. We can therefore be more effective at helping and healing others and also raise the vibration of the planet as a whole. This is already happening , the angels say that the number 444 is a significant number because 4 represents our base our stability a frame work in which to grow, $4 + 4 + 4 = 12$ which reduces to the vibration of 3 being associated with the holy trinity, or integration of mind body and spirit. You cannot access the higher divine energies until you have the frame work or base (stability). Once these chakras, lower or base, sacral and solar plexus energies are balanced then it is possible to create with intention and angelic wisdom.

Fallen Angels

The candle flickered an eternal flame

To remind us once again

That we could share its immortal glow

Spirits come and spirits go

I watched you fall away from me

Your heart so longed to be free

But you stayed entangled in a web

Life's illusions tears are shed

But you choose your pattern of life

Born again so you can strife

Bleeding deep through Christ's resurrection

Your spirit lost of all connection

We're trying to help you from our side

So you no longer need to hide

Spread forth the light

We'll come and aid

The Fallen as their memories Fade

ARE ANGELS REAL?

This was also included in my book the Silver Lining but I feel that it belongs in a book about angels because part of it is a direct channeling from the angels.

Sometimes people ask me about my angels and if I know their names. I have at times been aware of angels' names in my work. But I don't really feel it is necessary for me to know. I have often felt a presence working with me during a reading or healing, which to me is good confirmation that the angels are around. The name of anything, such as an angel, guide, or light worker only serves as a reminder that they are real to us. And with faith and love we often find it is not necessary to cling to this. Still, it is true that many people seem to like evidence. That is human nature. However, one of the most important aspects relating to angels is that angels are fantastic at the work they do and how much they help all of us in our lives. I believe that angels are one-dimensional beings (this means that they have mastered all the dimensions). I could have said "multidimensional," but they didn't want me to put it that way for some reason, as they are aware of all the dimensions. But their specific mission is to work with us, as they are indeed God's messengers. It's important to note that whilst writing this section of the book, the information I am receiving at this time is purely channeled rather than being my opinion:

Angels are aspects of us and aspects of God. Angels do not have the density of our vibration, so that they cannot exist on earth in the same way as we do. When we are born an angel is assigned to us as our keeper. We could say this angel is a "keeper of the light." Their job is to protect us from the darkness. It's not that darkness is ultimately bad for us, unless there is some sort of imbalance. If there is imbalance it means that we are stuck in a place where there is too much darkness. With each angel comes a book of promises, which is the soul contract you have made with your angel before you came into this density. Your angel acts as the higher aspect, or a more evolved you. And although a separate entity, its mission is very much just to guide you on your path.

The more light you receive from your angel by connecting to him or her (as they are both male and female); the easier it is for you to find your path back to God. By listening to the messages the angel whispers in your ear you are able to achieve your soul purpose more easily without going on too many diversions. The angel knows your soul purpose but has made a promise in the contract or book of promises that only one thing will be revealed to you at a time. This is to avoid complete confusion or mind overload. And hence you have gradual progression so that you can learn the basics first. People will come into your life who may challenge your thoughts and feelings and also your connection with your angel. This can be seen as a sort of gridlock as you move through the experience you have attracted. The experience you attract, although sometimes harsh, is to aid your growth and personal development and to ultimately gain wisdom.

Sometimes we feel as though we have lost the guidance and become almost lost souls, or lost at sea for a period of time, whilst we try to re-establish connection with our higher aspects or angel wisdom. Despite how alone, we may feel at times, our angel is still there listening to us. He or she is with us all the time.

Our own Guardian Angel loves us dearly but cannot break the contract of the book of promises because this is what we agreed to at the beginning. Some people refer to this as a soul contract that you agreed to before you came to Earth. In order for your angel to turn the next page so that you can realign and connect with your soul purpose, you must overcome the gridlock challenges of the darker aspects of yourself. Hence running away from them, along with anger, revenge, or lack of forgiving, never really solves a thing, and keeps us in a negative state. Hence we must learn to forgive and release in order to move forward. It is only through love and acceptance, and not through fighting or blaming others that we can find the universal love to reconnect. Your angel is then able to turn the next page of your book of promises and reveal the next step in your life along your path to enlightenment.

Of course your angels are there to assist you at every step of your life and asking for help is good. They do not intend to let you down. But without the challenges of the dark side of your nature there would be no duality, and therefore no need for balance. If the world were only full of light there would be no driving force to take us forward because it is through anger, frustration, and disappointments that we are often propelled forward. We need drive and inner strength to establish an even better connection for us, one where we are made aware our soul's purpose. Without the shadow, we would become just wishy-washy individuals with no soul experience.

If we permanently reside in the light, how could we ever get to grips with the world we live in or teach others if we had not experienced both? The light and the dark are all part of our evolvement on planet Earth. So in other words, you can sit in the dark for a while, but you must learn to turn on the light. Or you can be in the light for ages and become frustrated that there is no excitement or stimulation. However, shining a bit of light onto a situation can be illuminating and enable us to see more clearly what is going on. And this is certainly very useful if we are stuck in a void.

Feeling Stuck

Being stuck can certainly make you feel that we are being pulled further and further down. When this happens it may well be necessary to ask someone to shine a bit of light for you such as a therapist, healer, or close friend, whilst you link again to that higher aspect of yourself and learn to listen to your angel. You are not alone or shut out in your experience. You are only recoiling, becoming a tighter spring, ready to be propelled forward with more confident strides. Remember that an angel is a messenger, and as such gives you help and guidance rather than doing it all for you. On occasions when your life is in danger your angel can definitely help, and thus miracles can occur. This rather depends on your contract and what you have agreed upon on another level of existence. An angel will definitely intervene if she or he thinks that you still have important work to do on planet earth and you have just lost your way.

THE MATRIX OF ILLUSION

This part of the book could end up being extremely long and incorporate everything from politics, sovereignty, aliens, UFOs and much more! As this is a book primarily about angels I will aim to show you how the illusion is stopping us connecting to the higher part of us.

Much of the negativity and false media is being fed to us through the television, particularly in advertising, materialism and greed. What is happening is the chemical sabotage of our planet is preventing us remembering who we really are. It's a system that is designed to make us believe that 'not everything is possible' when an awful lot of that everything is! Many people will never reach their full potential because of their own limiting beliefs. Part of our self belief is trained out of us when we were children, by religion (belief in we are sinners) and also negative adults who no doubt have not evolved out of their own inner child issues. They find that their children are too difficult to deal with. In addition, this negativity is backed up by the beliefs of many 'systems' around us that no longer serve society! If we didn't do particularly well at school, and I am one of these people, it doesn't mean that the only choice for us is to work in a supermarket or be a cleaner! We have the power and the choice to re-train, or recognise our path in life or blue print. At any given moment in time, we have the opportunity to become aware of whom we are. Not our ego entity, our name or our job role but who we are, our uniqueness, our gifts and our talents. What is held within our hearts, our DNA structure and our human potential is a sovereign human being not a piece of fiction! However, sometimes the saboteur is so strong within us that we set ourselves up to fail. A dyslexic person can be very gifted. An autistic child may also have many gifts. Illusion as I see it, is a place where people have to fit into boxes, instead of being who they are, where jobs have been carved out to enable efficiency and money saving, to such a degree that the jobs have become 'soul less' and people robotic. We live in a society where so many people are bored sick and miserable being employed and the other half are bored sick and miserable being unemployed. Where young people fill themselves up with alcohol and drugs to numb themselves from the reality that being put in a box like this until the age of 65 is beyond depressing! Naturally, we would all be successful if it wasn't for the world, we live in and yes, we do have to live in the real world. But we live in a world that views academic intelligence as true intelligence, rather than getting to grips with the fact that emotional intelligence is true intelligence! Many academics (not saying all here) are only engaging with one half of the brain. They are so left brained that they are unable to connect with their creativity. It's the right brain which is the creative, which needs to be activated to gain balance. If you engage with both, then you really are a winner! But this involves applying your mind both strategically as well as creatively. I would like to think I had a little of both, having come from a secretarial administrative background and later trained as a therapist. Obviously writing, art, pottery, sculpturing, is all creative and many careers engage both sides of the brain. Being open minded is acceptance of right brained ideas!

It's hardly surprising that with all this going on, that what often happens is that you can emotionally give up. This is another part of the illusion or being stuck in the matrix. You did care once, when you were a child, you were vaguely aware of a good encouraging voice in your head but that was years ago. That voice went to sleep, you stopped listening. It could have been that someone told you that you were no good or perhaps plain stupid and that you believed them. That you were too fat, too short, not tall enough or you were clumsy. It could be that someone laughed horribly at you and you now no longer laugh yourself. There are many reasons why we get stuck in illusion, where the fantasy is better than the reality. Who would want to be awake when you can have your head stuck in soap opera, or in a computer game? You can be a fantasy character in Xbox with someone who has a much better life than you and you have the opportunity to imagine that their life is your life! When you can overspend and think you will figure it all out later. When you are up to your credit card limit but that's still alright because you are going to have the best holiday you have ever had! Who would actually want to be awake and aware and enjoy being in the NOW. If you did that then, you would have to face up to all the bad stuff as well as the good stuff. Being awake is a painful experience. Is meditation for people who are boring and aren't interested in a good life? No, it is not in fact people couldn't be more wrong! Meditation is for people who want to gain control of their life, focus their intentions and create a life which is really WOW!

ARCHANGELS MICHAEL, GABRIEL, RAPHAEL & URIEL

This section is about the archangels. Some of it I gained through my research into angels and some of it is channelled information given to me by the angels.

Each Archangel Angel has their own divine role and is also associated with specific colours and even crystals. We can utilise the powerful energies from the Archangels in our daily lives by asking them to come close to us.

Archangel Michael – Electric Blue – Divine Will and Joy

"Call upon me in times of fear. I will guide you through the many trials and tribulations of life by offering you my divine protection. See my light spiraling around you, keeping your safe. "I am with you." Michael's positivity very quickly transmutes our negative thoughts as well as dispelling the negative actions of others. Visualise him standing in front of you and ask for his divine protection. His sword of light has a powerful blue ray which brings in love, compassion and healing. It's known as the sword of truth. Archangel Michael asks that we learn to 'trust' in who we are by feeling the light of truth and honour (integrity). His sword of light guides us when we are lost. He illuminates our path and brings us out of darkness. He's by our side at times of need. He heals our hearts and brings in light love and compassion. Ask for him to be with you when fearful or alone especially when you going on any journey through life. He can also be called upon when going on a journey in your car. Some people say that his sword of light represents "Christ Consciousness." This energy has a high frequency energy which helps dissolve illusions and brings wisdom. His light of truth enables us to move forward by releasing. Christ consciousness is much evolved energy which is here now to help humanity evolve. This energy is accessible to anyone who asks. It is important for me to say that there are angels mentioned in many different religions and they do not belong solely to Christianity. For ease of purpose I have referred to the Angels as (him but they could just as easily be her).

We can call upon Archangel Michael to help release us from situations in life that no longer serve us. If you are finding it hard to move on from someone in your life, but you know in your heart that the situation isn't right he is always there to help.

Archangel Gabriel

Is known as bringer or messenger – primarily associated with compassion.

AFFIRMATION FOR GABRIEL BRINGER OR MESSENGER

Angel of Love and Compassion

I am an extension of Your Love

I am willing and open

I feel gratitude for my many blessings

Each day is a gift which enhances my life

Gabriel is the 8th Archangel. Gabriel with Michael rule over the etheric soul which give light to soul and body but astrologically he rules the moon (emotions of the soul) Cancer.

Gabriel is the source for our inspiration and imagination. He helps us express our creativity as he shines divine light and celebrates our individuality. Gabriel's energy is relentless as he guides humanity and points us in the right direction. At times we can feel like lost sheep but he is always there as a pillar of strength and encouragement. When we get stuck and don't know which way to turn he acts as a sign post for us and enables us move forward. He also helps with new creative ideas. His energy is very strongly associated with creation, birth and maternity. He helps our confidence and enables us to move forward with love and awareness. He is extremely strong and helps us to confront our own barriers and reflect upon our limiting beliefs! He is gentle kind and re-assuring and can also be called upon to comfort and heal our pain. I see Gabriel pointing his finger like a guiding star who is giving us both direction and wisdom. Trust in Gabriel as he can bring balance, inspiration and wisdom to us by showing us a clear way forward. He brings positive messages and assures us that it is safe for us to be powerful. He also helps us understand our dreams and enhances intuition and clairvoyance as Gabriel rules those going beyond the astral. He can be seen in the Tarot as blowing a trumpet on Judgment Day!

Rays Silver and Deep Blue- Planet Neptune

Crystal for confidence – Citrine

Dream recall – Red Jasper placed under the pillow

Archangel Raphael

The Healer – Integration

Angel of Healing

I seek you in times of need

To heal others and myself

I am open to your energies

I utilise them in my daily life

Raphael is better known as the angel of healing. He enables our chakras to receive more light while he assists us in our own healing process. Call upon him and you will soon feel the start of the integration of your body, mind and spirit. His main purpose is to renew and change. When we are prepared to leave the old behind, in comes the new. We won't always find it easy to make this transition because we may feel stuck or not worthy enough to make this giant leap of faith but Raphael understands our higher nature or divine self. He will send us powerful healing to help so that we can soon embrace the new. Archangel Raphael supports us during our healing by enhancing our intuition. When we feel we need a little assistance in difficult times, find a quiet place where you can sit and ask Raphael's healing energy to come into your space. You will soon notice a slight change in vibration and feel his love flowing towards you. This enables you to connect to your own intuition and to listen to your inner guidance.

The energy connected with Raphael is very strong and powerful and his healing transcends all time and space. He is extremely virtuous. He has emerald green light in his halo and he uses this green or emerald energy, to help with healing which is brilliant for balancing our heart chakra. We can ask Raphael to help us by visualizing his emerald green light, breathe it in slowly. As you breathe in the green light, you will be sending healing to your heart. He will also help us with our work, healing others. His main purpose is to release us from the bonds of the past by enabling our own energies to flow. He doesn't allow things to stagnate and when you ask for his healing energies, sometimes changes can be swift. The emerald green brings both clarity and illumination. He lights our path at the same time as holding the light for others. He heals both our emotional and physical bodies and he allows us to celebrate our spirit.

Crystals for Healing – Green Emeralds for our heart chakra, Rose Quartz for self love.

ARCHANGEL URIEL

Uriel – God is my Light -Divine Fire – Keeper of Earth Mysteries

Angel of Fire

You burn away my past.

As I let go, your flames cleanse my heart.

I rise up once again from the ashes to start anew

I am moving into transcendence

Uriel is both an Archangel and a Cherub or Seraph angel. His name means God is Light. He's above us and he oversees us. He is very responsible for our connection to planet earth. He helps us to resolve international conflicts such as war and on a much smaller scale he helps us with our inner conflicts. His teaching is about forgiveness. As he washes away our negativity as we learn to forgive others and ourselves (in religious terms this is known as repentance).

Uriel holds a disc of tarnished copper which reminds us of the stability of our connection through the earth. He represents our security and search for confidence and success. He's often seen as an emblem of a bull because he's extremely strong and determined there's no holding him back. He watches over thunder and terror and unleashes our inner wisdom. He's also both a hurricane and a calm sea. He's the angel of the southerly fair wind. He stands at the gate of Eden with his sword of fire. This archangel is very much connected to the elemental realms, or nature spirits, which restore harmony beauty and balance. He is also associated with electricity, fire and solar energy.

Uriel brings peace to us by instilling determination. If you are feeling annoyed, irritable or angry, he can help release this. Sometimes we really struggle to let go of a situation which no longer serve us. Situations can make us angry and this can lead us into volatile or unstable relationships. This angel's energy can help these feelings rise to the surface, so that they can be healed. He helps to clear the solar plexus and purifies energies which are out of harmony.

Archangel Uriel is also connected to transformation and alchemy. He awakens our own abilities by awaking us to manifestation. He brings insight, knowledge and illumination. He's particularly connected to the mental plane because encourages us to study and follow our spiritual path. By connecting with Archangel Uriel, we become aware of ideas and we can put those ideas into action. He helps us find the courage to move forward by transforming negative actions into positive and he gives us focus. Through connecting with his energy nothing remains hidden because it rises to the surface to be healed. We are able to think more clearly and our spiritual growth is accelerated. When we connect with Archangel Uriel we are blessed by his knowledge and wisdom. His energy provides an open channel which connects in to the higher planes of consciousness so we can co-create in love and understanding.

Planet – Uranus – metal - copper – his rays golden orange, rose and purple.

Crystals – Amethyst for intuition and perception and angelite which is used to connect to the wisdom of the angels.

LIGHT BEINGS

In the late eighties, my sister, who was very close to me, was dying of cancer and I was angry. She was only 28 and had her whole life in front of her. It was only right that she being so young, should live because she hadn't had the chance to complete her mission or life. I know that many of you will not doubt be able to associate with my feelings about this at that time, because losing someone at a young age, is very hard for anyone. However spiritually accepting you are, when it comes to losing someone close, it doesn't seem to become any easier the more it happens. In my late twenties, when I was losing my sister, I desired to know about the existence of God. Not through any spiritual medium, nor through my experiences of the Catholic Church when I was a child, but through my own experience. Through having some kind of evidence that there was such a place or experience that we refer to as heaven. So one day, shortly before the death of my sister, I literally shouted at God with all the force of my being. Which like I explained to you, is not really necessary, because for us to ask our angels is enough to be heard. For me though, at the time, I wanted to shout. I was angry and I was disillusioned and I wanted to know why this so called God was not doing enough to save my sister. How could he be so cruel, and if a miracle was to happen I wanted it to happen NOW. My desire was so strong that I literally forced the energy outwards with all my being. My cells filled up with the intention. I moved out of expectation because I had none. My only desire was to find out what there was. Was there a place, a time, a heaven? I allowed it to be shown to me in whatever form it chose to show itself.

I was dressed in a white robe. Surprisingly I could see many robed beings all shining with light. They were smiling at me and I felt calm and happy. Some of the beings were walking quietly together but two came towards me to lead me up some steps. I looked down at my clothes and I noticed that I too was wearing a white robe. I could see the folds of the material but I accepted it without question. There were many marble pillars. I stretched out to touch them and they felt cold to the touch. I was aware that I was in another dimension perhaps a dimension of light? I happily walked up the steps with the two light beings. I felt comforted and in total acceptance. Then I heard a voice say "she's ready now!" I somehow knew that I was ready, but I didn't understand where the voice came from! I found myself standing on some sort of a platform where a huge expanse of light shone down on me. The light was totally absorbing. It took me to a place of peace beyond anything I had known on earth. I was in complete surrender. I looked up to the sky and saw that the beam stretched on forever up into the heavens. I was glowing.

I opened my eyes and I saw that it was 4 am. I was still glowing like a radiant being and I couldn't move. I looked at my body and I was in a cocoon. If anything it looked similar to being an Egyptian mummy but I was not only cocooned in white robes but I could see myself glowing. This went on for the next two hours but I gradually found that I could move again. When I arose from bed around 6 am I found that I was completely energised. I was no longer the same person. Yes I was ready. I was ready to understand the light. I found that the light was transformational and I knew that the light could also be used for healing. When we heal it's just another extension of this Universal light, the light of the creation. It is also the light of our divine spark, the intention of who we are. We were ignited by our parents in their love which is given by our creators. How then can we not be creative? How then could we not be in touch with our divine spark, or feel that the world is flat and angels, bringers of the light don't exist? Heaven is a sunbeam!

So in this world we are cocooned. We are the chrysalis waiting to turn into the butterfly, the more light that we absorb, the lighter we become to the point of luminescence. Earth is a playground for our soul's evolution so that we can be magnificent, living in our own splendor. Each one of us has lived many lives trying to break free from our cocoon (the illusion) that prevents us from fully connecting to the power or our eternal light. We have chosen to be here in order to learn and through our chakra system we are able to absorb more light, raise our vibration and come into alignment with the earth's energetic grid. We are able to connect to the vast matrix of light which surrounds planet earth. We are each of us a conductor of this light. When our chakras are balanced open and spinning we are a conduit for positive energies. Not only do we influence people around us, we also charge the earth under our feet. Many ancient buildings, particularly churches were built on these energy lines that are commonly known as ley lines. The two important ley lines that run the length of England are called the Michael and Mary Lines.

The Michael and Mary ley lines link St Michael's Mount (Cornwall), Stonehenge, Aylesbury and Hopton (Suffolk), passing through a number of other towns including the Abbey in Bury St Edmunds. People often notice strong energies on these lines which can have healing properties. They also link sacred sites such as Stonehenge Avebury and Glastonbury Tor. Many people visit these places every year. This isn't just for historical interest, but they actually find that the energies of these places are extremely uplifting. I particularly like Castlerigg in the Lake District, which is an amazing stone circle. From the stones you can see a panoramic view of the mountains particularly Blencathra which is my favourite mountain. It is commonly known as 'Saddleback' because the top of it is shaped like a horse's saddle. It has a rugged charm, I feel matched by no other, and the charm of this particular mountain made me returns to the Lake District again and again, staying in Threkeld at the foot of the mountain.

So the energy or the frequency of a place is important, because when the energy is good, you can experience a really uplifting feeling. But it is also possible that you can the complete opposite, a pull you down feeling as I felt when I visited the museum in Boscastle. Like I said, it depends what resonates with you because all of us are different. I've actually been to the Museum twice because I felt it was so interesting. Stone circles could well have been built as early places of worship but have we ever got our head around the true purpose for building them? Perhaps they were some sort of early navigation system for Neolithic spacecraft seen from outer space, akin to our modern day landing strips which can easily be seen miles in the air.

This is a message which I received a few years ago from Archangel Gabriel Bringer of Light which reminds us where we are on our voyage of discovery and I feel gives us information about where we are headed!

As more of you begin to expose the truth, the light is starting to emerge. This is indeed the dawn of the Age of Aquarius where there will be no formal instruction on how to move forward in your life but unusual and differing approaches will lead the way. Do not stagnate because movement within you, however little, contributes to movement of the whole. We are aiding this process but we cannot do it for you. We bring the light of illumination which is not just the light of your soul but guides the earth through the next evolutionary stage. Do not believe everything that you hear because there are many so called 'prophets' who will try and lead you away from the truth held in your hearts. There is safety in numbers. It isn't that you cannot make it alone, but you need to work in groups to bring in the different energetic patterns needed for transformation. Standing in formation will help bring about the new energetic structures for planet earth. She is constantly reshaping and reforming but her central core is still, as yours should be now. Your re-actions are crucial on a physical level to holding her steady and guiding her like a ship into port. We are sending love and light as the illusions fall away. What you thought or considered to be safe is no longer where you are able to seek comfort. There is comfort in still and contemplation in silence. We urge you to go within and seek solace. We cannot begin to explain to you on a human level why this is happening but we can ask you to trust in the process.

Certain souls at this time are bravely treading the way for a brave new world. They are path seekers they seek the light beyond the darkness. They know the inner calling of mother earth and what she is saying. The variations in frequencies will soon be felt as one internal sound or pulse. The pulse or heart beat of the mother will resonate within to keep us consciously aligned to the truth. It is distinctive and it is a sound not heard before as it differs in frequency to previous sounds coming from the mother. Those who are able to adapt to the new frequencies will find the transformation easy. It is natural for them to move with the ebb and flow and understand the bigger picture. It may feel as if you are pushed to the edge of sanity in your effort to understand why. So much has been hidden and we angels also have a full scale battle on our hands against the dark forces which enslave planet earth. This is only temporary. We do not work alone. There are many beings that will aid and assist us. When you look out from your 'port hole' of life the sea looks rough but from a multidimensional perspective, the wave is breaking. As it smashes on the rocks, energy is showered in so many different directions. It transforms the landscape. Everything that was once dark is now glistening. Every stone transformed into a shining jewel of truth and love. We cannot say that the sea is not going to get rough. We cannot promise that transformation is not a painful and necessary process. We will stand by you and help awaken those souls who have chosen to experience this truth. We give comfort to those who cannot be part of what lies ahead. We are assisting every human being on the planet right now, not just those who believe in us to make a conscious choice.

ANGELIC MEDITATIONS

I have decided to include some Angelic Meditations in this book to enable you to connect to your Guardian Angel. We must remember that angels are here for our greater purpose and for the greater good of humanity. Some of these meditations will be light but are designed for you to connect to a different type of energy and to open you up to new possibilities. By taking time to do these exercises you will be able to clear the solar plexus chakra thus enabling you to re-connect to your power centre and the central core of who you are. Detaching from people who have taken power from you both physically and emotionally is very important. We often let go of someone on the physical level but remain corded to them on an emotional level. Both of these exercises will really help you release and move on by letting go of negative energies and to put it simply bringing your energy back to you by re-connecting with your soul fragments to become integrated. We are here to integrate to be complete and whole. Then we find balance, happiness and fulfillment through our inter-actions with others and life is joyful instead of hard work.

Call upon the Angel of Reflection and the Angel of Laughter

You are the Inner Light I seek

I feel my Divine Spark Within

I am connected to the process of Life

My beauty is found on Reflection

An Angel sits beside a pond of flowing water. As she gazes into the water, the water becomes clear, a perfect mirror for us to reflect and heal. The Angels say that when someone starts to mirror our behaviour, or a negative situation keeps repeating, it is an opportunity for self healing and transformation. We need to reach deep into ourselves through our third chakra, our solar plexus which is about two inches above the naval. This chakra which is yellow, it's our power centre. It's associated with issues of self worth. When it is in alignment, it helps us find balance and gives us the power to create and manifest. This is a chakra not to be ignored as it can help us manifest dreams into reality.

There are one or two things we need to look at here. Where is your power, your own power, right now?

Are you completely in your own power or are you giving away your power to another person or a situation such as a past relationship or an old energy pattern. It could be that the person or situation no longer serves your higher purpose but you are still connected to it, fearing to move forward in your life. The Angel of Reflection is here to help you. Someone could be making you angry and you feel out of control because they are pushing all your buttons. Perhaps it is time to look into your heart because there may be things to heal, forgive or release that you haven't been totally aware of. Ask the Angels to help you with the releasing process.

Forgiveness is found through reflection and it is also a gateway, that once opens, allows rushes of positive new energy into your heart. Wear yellow or visualise a bright strong yellow sun within the solar plexus. Wearing yellow or using appropriate crystals also sends light to your power centre and helps you stay aligned with the wonderful person that you are. Be the powerful and creative individual as it was intended. Feel how good it is to be free of others manipulations.

The angels say that the truth is painful but there is no hiding from our mirrors. Sometimes the image of who we are can be distorted in this dimension but your soul knows the truth. See the distortion, walk into the hall of mirrors and look around. Are things different to how you imagined? Are you ready to get a clear image of who you really are and what you want in your life? Or are you holding on too tightly to old and outdated ideas and concepts. Are you ready to heal your heart and be in truth and shine your own light? Cords from the solar plexus need releasing and there is a strong need to let go. There is also a necessity for laughter because fun and laughter are great natural healers. How long is it since you laughed and really let those barriers down? Feel the energy rising in your belly and spreading out like a bright sun throughout your body. Experience the sheer joy of a child on Christmas Day opening his or her presents or jumping over the waves, as your feet sink into the cold wet sand. Call upon the Angel of Laughter and the Angel of Reflection because they will guide you on the wonderful journey into your soul. Let go of hatred and stress, cleanse and dance!

Angel of Laughter

I overflow with an Abundance of Joy

Which I wish to share with others

Let us laugh and smile

And be as little children

The Oasis

Close your eyes and take some long deep breaths relax your whole body. Breathe out stale and old energy and imagine breathing in strong golden sunlight. With each breath, you become lighter and brighter until you begin to glow like a ray of golden sunshine. Keep breathing and imagine the suns beautiful rays shining down on you. Then visualise a small pool of water, it could be an oasis in the desert surrounded by cool tropical plants. Visualise yourself naked entering the pool via some small marble steps.   Swim around the pool and enjoy yourself. The water is warm and bubbly and the bubbles want to make you giggle. When you feel completely ready walk up the little tiny steps and out of the pool and feel you feet on the warm sand. There is a beautiful angel holding a clean white towel for you. Put the towel around you and feel the warmth of the tropical sun.

Thank the Angel

Associated crystals: Yellow or Golden Calcite stimulates the will and citrine for confidence and power and abundance.

ORDERS OF ANGELS

Although in biblical and historical terms angels are quite orderly and divided into Hierarchy. People see angels in many different ways. The fact that we see them with wings is basically because they're God's messengers, but equally we could see angels as twinkles of light or even an abstract pattern."

The Angels tell me that they chatter a lot which I find quite interesting. I feel that there is much discussion between angels deciding whether we take them seriously. If in fact we do take them seriously then certainly they will listen to our prayers.

The Hierachy of Angels

Why, are Angels here now and why are so many people seeing them?

I believe that the angels that are visiting us at the moment are bringing important messages. They are appearing to so many of us because they are helping us evolve to the fourth dimension.

The Angels lift us to a higher dimension of awareness and they help us let go of illusions. Once we are able to see things from a higher perspective, negative thoughts no longer have the same power or hold us. We are able to move on from where we no longer desire to be! This is mainly done through the power of intention, thy will be done, but it is not an easy journey. It is certainly difficult alone and we all need guidance, help and understanding on our respective paths. The angels are literally giving us wings so that we can soar to greater heights and be the humans we really want to be. Through angelic help and wisdom, we can be free of hurt and illusion. We can reconnect to love and understanding of our self and one another. It's a difficult transition process. It's also apparent that some people do not want to accept the new spiritual truths that the angels are bringing to us. Even if we do accept it on some level, we need to let go of some ideas that we have held very dear to our hearts. Moving into the higher dimensions is not only a joyous process but indeed one of self discipline.

Angels have come to work with individuals and also through consciousness as a whole. Many messages are channelled this way and that is why several people may say the same thing at the same time but in slightly different ways. The Angels are making an imprint on consciousness as a whole.

As the Seraphim's keep saying to me that they want to be heard, I will explore them in a little more detail. The Seraphim guard God's throne (traditional interpretation). I am being told that their energy is bright blue and is often associated with royalty. They do not act as messengers because they are heavenly hosts which entertain The Gods. I personally do not believe in God on a throne but it could be symbolic of the high energies associated with God. They also support us by invoking the violet flame and the clearing away of negative energies because they are protectors of the earth. If you call upon the violet flame of St. Germain these angels are in abundance. They literally dance with the flames and sing. You may have heard them singing, it sounds like a quiet whistling or hissing noise. They are protectors and they help to keep the energies on planet earth clean and pure. They are not interested in helping on a one to one, or personal missions with you but they are concerned with humanity as a whole, particularly anything that is out of balance. They are guardians and they are also educators. In addition they are stunningly beautiful and sometimes appear as geometric shapes. They link with Pythagoras and sacred geometry, attaching themselves to the energies of higher wisdom and learning. Their divine light reaches out to many individuals if you visit places which have held their vibration throughout history such the Sistine Chapel. I am also told that they are in abundance at the pyramids. They cleanse on a big scale with a vibration which is regal in essence.

EARTH ANGELS, ASCENSION AND METATRON.

The angels are very busy helping us to not only heal ourselves, but they are also busy cleansing the environment in which we live. One of their main tasks during our present evolutionary period is to raise our vibration. To explain this in greater detail I have decided to add some information which I received in May of last year which is becoming more relevant as time goes on.

"In the beginning, at the time of our separation, we grieved for the loss of you because we could not hold your density. Our frequencies are attuned like a tuning fork and you could not exist within the infinite as us because of a strong desire to experience all that there is on the earth plane. The separation then began. We now come to individuals on the planet which can connect with us, at our desired frequency. It is hard for you humans to keep the channel open and often we find that the channels are temporarily sealed that we wish to pass the information along. We have to therefore choose other avenues to alert you and we appear to symbolically have wings as depicted in the scriptures and in art but the wings only resemble your need for time and space. There is no such thing as time in our

vibration of love. We are constantly trying to show you humans this by making watches and clocks stop but you do not seem to understand. Time is meaningless, it is density. Once again we remind you of your abilities to slip in and out of the frequencies like us using only linear time and space time which is not the same as earth's physical time."

One thing that is very interesting at the moment is that it almost appears as if time is speeding up. We have got to a stage where we are chasing our tails so much that sometimes we find it hard to just stop and be in the 'present' which is the angels gift to us! The angels say in order for us to connect to them, we must learn how to be still once again and be in the now.

"Our mission on earth is nearly complete and we are working to raise the vibration consciousness as a whole. Whilst the earth may appear dark, individuals have more light in which to spread. We need you to help us with our mission to spread the light we are betwixt the earth dimensions working as you earthlings say interactively, to bring the information forward which is necessary for the changeover".

Another thing which is very interesting is that as humans interact with angels more and more and learn of the beautiful gifts open to humanity, they will find it easier to manifest blessings into their lives. We will soon find it easy and common place to manifest things that we want in our lives with the help of the angels. Cosmic ordering will become common knowledge especially with children. The rainbow, indigo and crystal children know how to cosmic order naturally and will lead the way by showing the older generation how it is done. Call in the Angel of Manifestation to bring bright blessings into your life. Not only are angels showing me where to park now instantly, but they are also sending me people with half used car parking tickets!

Angels of Wisdom

The Cherubs bring wisdom to us by spreading light from the God source. They are also the guardians of the heavens and stars. I often see their sweet little faces peaking at me and I can tell you that they also laugh at us a lot like children especially when we get things wrong!

There are also Angels of Clarity which bring vision and illumination and Angels of Intention which relate very strongly to desire energy. Ask for these angels to come to you when you want to gain insight into something or start a new project along with the Angel of Strength as they are here to help you.

How to call in the Angels of Wisdom (gold/royal purple):-

Angels of Wisdom

I now move through my life lessons with ease

I acknowledge new learning as I see new

opportunities appearing in my life

with synchronicity and understanding

Help me understand my path more clearly

and release the things that no longer serve me

- ➤ Remember call the Angels in through belief and desire
- ➤ Keep requests in the now
- ➤ Use a clear crystal for clarity
- ➤ Know that the angels have heard your request

Guardian Angels

Your Guardian Angel is with you all the time and if you learn to develop a conversation with your angel, the messages will become much stronger.

> ➤ Angels appreciate us calling them by their name.
> ➤ They do not have free will like us as they are God's messengers.
> ➤ They are God's servants and as such they are obedient messengers and do not bend rules!
> ➤ They cannot go against the freewill of another individual.

Archangel Metatron and his significance.

Metatron is a very different Archangel because he was originally thought to be the Prophet Enoch and he was basically transformed into an Archangel by God. His name comes from a Latin name Metator, which means guide or measurer. He is the head of the world of creation which feels very appropriate as we learn to manifest (create) blessings into our own lives.

He is associated with sacred geometry and also with the activation of our 12th strand of DNA. Many of the things we see in our world now are illusionary. One of these is the feeling that we can achieve happiness with things solely outside of us. In geometric terms Metatron is complete (Metatron's cube) and does not need anything outside in order to be, which in simple terms, creates a "spiral of light." Human beings will enter the spiral when they learn to let go of their ego (a need to identify with roles or things) and become more at-one with who they really are.

The essential Metatronic pattern is the 3D form "The Flower of Life" which I personally refer to as the Mystic Rose. This flower brings focus, balance and harmony through the heart chakra and also brings all the other chakras into alignment. Metatron's cube has often been drawn around a person to protect them from dark energies. It is good to visualise for protection along with other sacred geometry symbols. Putting yourself inside a crystal whilst meditating can have a similar effect. When we are balanced, we are ready to manifest. Call in Archangel Metatron for inner transformation, alignment, cosmic ordering and ascension! Gabriel is the 8th Archangel Gabriel with Michael's help rule over the etheric soul, which gives light to soul and body but astrologically he rules the moon, which is ruled by Cancer.

Crystals – Amethyst for perception, Angelite to connect to the wisdom of the angels and sapphires for cleansing, illumination and purity.

CHRIST CONSCIOUSNESS AND DNA

The 12th stand of the DNA is our connection between our consciousness and the mass or Christ consciousness. Christ's final integration into our hearts is given as a gift to humanity through the various channels or portals opening up on planet earth. We eagerly await the return of Christ to our hearts through the new frequencies. A new sound of platinum frequency is elevating our soul consciousness out of the astral which has previously sabotaged our emotional bodies to the 4th dimension of love, wisdom and peace.

Christ's integration is available to all souls on the earth who are ready to receive and who connect deep within their hearts. The DNA activation is made through the ll.ll gateways, where conscious time lapses to cause reversals of earth time, giving a synapse or moment in time to allow the energies to filter subconsciously into our energy fields. Through these moments of extreme awareness we are able to access the NOW moment or seed of God more easily and start to plant the seeds for our New Earth.

In order to do this, we must try and keep in awareness as much as possible by the eating of healthy food, taking regular exercise and making time to be you. The platinum frequency is transformational and cleansing. It also ignites the sacred flame of St. Germain installing within you the graciousness of God. The flame which is created by this frequency is 728 hertz which is God Divine. We must transcend the ego in order to access the portals of new vibration or frequencies which are already open on planet earth. We do need to be free of sin but we need to recognise that sin is only symbolic, as is love because ultimately we are pure divine energy which is that of creation. We need to move out of judgment and engage in surrender. We are in essence holy and divine but our illusion or ego self keeps us in a place of introspection. We constantly look for comparisons of a measure of 'how we are doing in life.' When we move past the ego part of us, we are released. We are no longer in the vibration of our thoughts mastering us. We are in surrender and acceptance, receiving angelic light through our heart. Many talk now of ancestral memory and suggest that we literally hold the karma for our ancestors. Some of you may have chosen to clear your ancestral lineage in this lifetime. The angels say that we do not hold the responsibility for others although attitudes and belief patterns may be generational and held within your DNA. As you clear your energy fields by integrating the higher frequencies bestowed on planet earth, you are in effect clearing the mass energy of humanity as a whole, but there is no responsibility for your ancestors. Saying that through the thought form that like attracts like, we have many ancestral memories which are not living in the past but coherently exist in many dimensions of your truth. When we hold on to a concept or 'truth' we then integrate this truth into our energy field and start to live it. It soon becomes your reality or experience. For what you believe you attract and as you attract so you believe. Therefore you very soon have supporting evidence for your beliefs that back you up all the way. To release from this truth stand point, then becomes exceedingly difficult and if you have ancestral karma, you have ancestral karma, because that's your reality. The situation is playing out and therefore you are continually provided with evidence to support this. This could well be one of your soul lessons or a soul contract that you agreed to, before you ascended on planet earth. For other souls, the attractions which they manifest are very different. Their mission or blue print is unique. For some of us this may feel quite alien. Not understanding or knowing where that person is coming from, or feeling that they have got it wrong because they lack understanding is hard but we must not lose sight of the fact that each soul is unique. When you are in a 'release' of some description it's a multi dimensional experience and we want to hold on to what is comfortable and familiar. Perhaps the way that you dealt with a situation before because was successful in essence, from a 3D perspective. But now you have to re-visit a similar situation from a 4th dimensional perspective where there is only pure love and divine wisdom and you need to rise above it. This often involves forgiveness rather than avoidance! In this dimension there is no judgment and ultimately nothing to work through, apart from acknowledging that the experience is merely a mirror. It is part of us, a soul fragment asking to be healed and integrated into the whole being. The illusions which we create were created so that we can break through, and understand that our connection is all that there is. We are just an aspect of the continuum of love, peace and understanding and this energy is vast. Not only does it encompass planet earth but many other solar systems which match earth's particular vibration. So if you sometimes feel like you have been in another place, you may have been because your physical counterpart is currently in this time and space but your energy counterpart is multi dimensional and has no earth bound restrictions. Gravity is in essence created for the physical body but not for the energetic or ethereal which is divinely connecting to the larger part of the whole! It is time to catch up!

ON A SOUL LEVEL WE ARE ALL EQUAL

"As you reach the top of your mountain, remember you have just been the person walking behind."

The more we become aware of who we are on a deeper and perhaps more profound level of awareness, the less relevance other people's opinions have on us. Our soul's evolution becomes one of truth and understanding. Do others opinions really matter? Are we using others opinions as a 'yard stick' for our spiritual growth? In my experience being influenced by others has certainly become a thing of the past. There are no levels. It could be argued in biblical terms that "my father's house has many mansions" is an acknowledgement of these divisions. Do we create these divisions by not connecting to the truth and light of our soul? How do we as humans see these different levels of existence? Are they upper, middle or lower or set on a scale of frequencies? Is the vibration of energy or matter simultaneously creating situations in order for our own soul growth? Are our experiences so unique that another's energy pattern is only serving to highlight our own need for yet more spiritual learning? Do we think we are climbing an ascension ladder where anyone who gets in our way, will be used as a step to get to where we feel that we want to go? Or is this our ego acting out yet another scenario which is showing us that we are no more evolved than the next person?

When I was a child we had many jigsaw puzzles but the one which was my favourite was called 'The Post Office'. I loved this jigsaw. It had familiar friendly faces of people queuing and chatting. However, the most appealing thing about it was that it didn't actually have any sky, filling in the sky on a jigsaw always felt too hard for me to achieve. In my eyes, one piece of the sky looked completely identical to the next. I felt that it was an impossible task and one which would be too difficult to complete alone. Each piece of the jigsaw was completely individual. Yet each tiny piece of the sky appeared to look the same. In reality, each piece had to be different in order to make up the whole. Each interlocking section undoubtedly had its own merit. which I refused to see because the challenge of identifying these slight differences were something I did not want to comprehend let alone engage with. Many of us have had the experience of feeling of "I know this already." We often make assumptions.

Assumptions I have found are generally unhealthy. We can easily get frustrated by others lack of understanding of a situation which seems to us quite obvious. It is easy for us to fall into an assumption about somebody rather than to find out the truth. Although people and situations often appear the same, they are often most definitely not. Often something only becomes obvious to us because it is in "our experience" we have developed knowledge from being privileged enough to receive that experience. We may not view it as a privilege because it may have caused us pain. On reflection though and with hindsight, we often feel that we have gained and often we offer these experiences to others. They become pointers or inner directions that we share with others when we talk about lessons learnt!

As you climb your mountain remember you have been the person behind! There will always be someone in front of you! When you do finally reach your perceived top, you may well find that the person you considered behind got there long before you (tortoise and hare). Do we ever know what challenges another person has to face because each person we encounter on our path holds a very different and valuable piece of sky? We can't assume that we'll see their sky! Interesting enough, my younger sister always enjoyed the sky. It was logical for her to work at the most difficult first. I however would only be comfortable starting in the middle and then working outwards to the four corners. I always struggled with the top. The top row represented the highest and the most challenging section of the puzzle to complete. Sometimes we feel that we have had made good headway and then we see that we forgot about something three rows back. Was there something that someone had exchanged with us in the past that we missed? A lesson not learned because our blinkered view was one of he or she is not in the same place as me. Everything in your life has value from the mundane to the sometimes ridiculous. Appreciate the gifts which people bring and share because our soul needs to experience. Our soul has to learn by its understanding of others experiences as well as our own.

If we come into this life with an individual set or

circumstances unique to us, then we are going to get individual reactions to those 'set of circumstances.' We are all unique in the way we live our game of life. One person may handle a situation completely different to the next person but does that make it better or worse? Are their soul lessons the same as ours? Personally I believe that there are many roads to Rome. As we are all equal on a soul level it is worth bearing in mind that honouring another's individuality however diverse, may be essential to our Soul's growth. It could be a corner filled that you previously could not complete. You may have helped to complete their corner. Soul groups evolve together. Not necessarily at the same time and the same space but they still evolve together. If you recognise something that irritates you in another, then it is likely that something similar irritates you about yourself. Your inner thoughts reflected in your outer reality.

Like one flint striking the other – a spark of recognition perhaps polar opposites finding that central point of balance where you become aligned with truth.

Creating our new earth - angel message

We realise that it is a very confusing time for you all. But remember that you made the choice to be here during the transition to light. It is literally as if one pole is set off against the other and the magnetic force between them is causing everything else to go out of alignment, a battle of opposing forces not just within the earth but within yourselves.

Many of you may experience distortions of vision at this time. It would appear as if the shutter has shut half way through an image before that image can be developed. We are creating your new earth – have vision. If you shut off now, you'll see nothing but a black line as images blur together creating greater distortion.

What is your vision? How do you see your new world? Hold your visions so that they can be re-framed in synchronicity love and understanding. You are contributing to the mass consciousness blue print of time space reality. It was decided thousands of years ago by your energy counterparts that we would come to this point in creation. We implore you to stay with what is in yourself at this time not out of you. You are all Gods' sons and daughters. We welcome you to our loving fold.

Visualising our New Earth

If you were going to create heaven on earth
how would it be?
We can create it you and me
We can be part of a brand new dream

Where the water is pure and beautifully clean
Where the people are joined together
Not through fear but through loves endeavour
Where there is no need for money because
everything is free
Because everything has value -
it is plain to see
There is no 'welfare state' because we all know what
to do
Offer a bed or divide things in two
Remember the story of the loaves and the fishes
in your heart it fulfils your deepest wishes
of abundance which grows and grows
not duality or separation which steps on your toes
 There is no pollution because people are content
to stay where the grass is green and need no
stories to invent
To realise that what they have is bountiful and pure
Everyone is wealthy
No longer is there poor
There are no weapons of mass destruction
There is no terrorist of minds invention
There is no fear of the an unknown threat
The veil is lifted the button is re-set
Time has started from zero point
We can't repeat we can only annoint
Bless this world and all who are part
Release the past and heal her heart

Does she have forgiveness so we can start afresh
Can you have forgiveness and release from this mess
Can we envisage and intend a better place
Even though we know that we have fallen from grace
Anything is possible we have the power
not just to ruin strip and devour
We have the power to heal
and the power to intend
It is our choice our voice that we send
Is the earth listening - does she have ears
Listen to you and then if becomes clear
Listen to you and hear the hum
The tone the note we have already begun ...

The new earth is unfolding but it is not without pain and sacrifice. The mother has love for every single being on the planet at this time but many of you seek to damage her physical existence. She is erupting and with this eruption comes renewal.

We are intelligent beings we hold your light and bring you comfort. We understand things from the human perspective and we know that it is no easy challenge to transcend what you may have felt was right but we urge you to connect into your heart, the centre of your love energy. Many talk of preparedness. We urge you to listen to yourself at this time. We would like to give you clearer directions but until the vision or 'unified field' of consciousness becomes stable then it is hard for us to polarize ourselves in order to see the many aspects and differences, within your human perspectives! We are beings of light, in order for you to embrace the seed of truth, which lies deep within your conscious human counterpart, it may be necessary for you to literally sprout your own seeds.

There are many seeds planted and within this book there are also seeds. There can be seeds of positivity and seeds of doubt. Do not throw your seeds upon the land and walk away. Seeds need to be loved and watered. You are your own wealth no money held within your hand is going to help you in times to come. Love is from within and it is eternal. It's enfolding, enveloping and divine. We ask you to seek your soul your spirit and trust that the earth will not turn to dust but it will shine like beads of light held within a vast eternal pool of knowledge, the pool that created by divine beings that inhabit the earth which you call humans. We watch your thoughts glisten like stars upon the rocks and the waves that hit the shore ignite them. We know the workings of your soul and we send love to all who seek us but most of all we ask that you love each other for the love of God is held within the heart of man or wo(man) within the womb of humanity or mother earth. We are one.

Made in the USA
Charleston, SC
08 October 2015